NISTIR 7731

Bicubic B-Spline Surface
Approximation of Invariant Tori

I0413125

S. Ramamurti
D. Gilsinn
Information Technology Labortory
Applied and Computational Mathematics Division

October 2010

U.S. Department of Commerce
Gary Locke, Secretary

National Institute of Standards and Technology
Patrick D. Gallagher, Director

Bicubic B-Spline Surface Approximation of Invariant Tori

Sita Ramamurti[*]
David E. Gilsinn[†]

October 14, 2010

Abstract

The invariant torus of a coupled system of Van der Pol oscillators is approximated using bicubic B-splines. The paper considers the case of strong nonlinear coupling. In particular, the shapes of invariant torii for the Van der Pol coupling parameter λ are computed in the range [0.1, 2.0]. Comparisons are given with results obtained by the MATLAB differential equation solver ode45. Very good normed residual errors of the determining equations for the approximate tori for the cases $\lambda = 0.1$, 0.6 are shown. At the upper limit of $\lambda = 2.0$ memory errors occured during the optimization phase for solving the determining equations so that full optimization for some knot sets was not achieved, but a visual comparison of the resulting invariant torus figure showed a close similarity to the solution using ode45.

Keywords: bicubic B-splines; determining equations; invariant torus; large parameter case; optimization; Van der Pol oscillators

1   Introduction

Physical problems involving coupled vibrating systems often lead to ordinary differential equations of the form

$$\ddot{\mathbf{x}} + \mathbf{A}\mathbf{x} = \lambda \mathbf{N}(\mathbf{x}) \tag{1}$$

where $\mathbf{x} \in \mathbf{R}^n$, $\mathbf{A}$ is diagonal, and $\mathbf{N}$ is a nonlinear function of $\mathbf{x}$. λ is a parameter that scales the nonlinearity. There are many forms of solutions to systems like (1), but we are interested in approximating a particular class of solutions. In particular, we are interested in systems that exhibit an invariant surface of solutions. That is a surface on which, if a solution passes through a point on the surface, then the entire solution remains on the surface. In the case of periodic solutions the surface is sometimes referred to as an invariant torus. In the case of small parameters there is a large literature on the existence and approximation of invariant tori (see e.g. Bogoliubov and Mitropolsky [1], Hale [9, 10], and Gilsinn [5]). For the case of a large parameter there is not much in the way of literature. The work of Ge and Leung [4] showed that the Fast Fourier Transform could be used as a tool to approximate invariant tori in the large nonlinearity case. In this study we introduce a bicubic B-spline computational algorithm that, at least for a certain class of nonlinear systems, computes invariant tori to a high degree of accuracy for a larger range of parameters. In

---

[*]Department of Mathematics, Trinity Washington University, Washington D. C. 20017, ramamurtis@trinitydc.edu

[†]Applied and Computational Mathematics Division, Information Technology Laboratory, National Institute of Standards and Technology, Gaithersburg MD 20899-8910, david.gilsinn@nist.gov.

1

particular, following the work of Gilsinn [6, 7], we shall consider the system of coupled Van der Pol oscillators

$$
\begin{aligned}
\ddot{x}_1 + \mu_1^2 x_1 &= \lambda(1 - x_1^2 - \alpha_1 x_2^2)\dot{x}_1, \\
\ddot{x}_2 + \mu_2^2 x_2 &= \lambda(1 - \alpha_2 x_1^2 - x_2^2)\dot{x}_2,
\end{aligned}
\tag{2}
$$

where μ_1/μ_2 are irrational multiples.

Under the change of coordinates $x_1 = r_1^{1/2}\sin(\mu_1\omega_1)$, $\dot{x}_1 = \mu_1 r_1^{1/2}\cos(\mu_1\omega_1)$, $x_2 = r_2^{1/2}\sin(\mu_2\omega_2)$, and $\dot{x}_2 = \mu_2 r_2^{1/2}\cos(\mu_2\omega_2)$ this system becomes

$$
\begin{aligned}
\dot{\omega}_1 &= 1 + \lambda\left(-\frac{1}{\mu_1}\right)\left(\sin(\mu_1\omega_1)\cos(\mu_1\omega_1) - r_1\sin^3(\mu_1\omega_1)\cos(\mu_1\omega_1)\right. \\
&\quad \left. -\alpha_1 r_2\sin(\mu_1\omega_1)\cos(\mu_1\omega_1)\sin^2(\mu_2\omega_2)\right), \\
\dot{\omega}_2 &= 1 + \lambda\left(-\frac{1}{\mu_2}\right)\left(\sin(\mu_2\omega_2)\cos(\mu_2\omega_2)\right. \\
&\quad \left. -\alpha_2 r_1\sin^2(\mu_1\omega_1)\sin(\mu_2\omega_2)\cos(\mu_2\omega_2) - r_2\sin^3(\mu_2\omega_2)\right)\cos(\mu_2\omega_2), \\
\dot{r}_1 &= 2\lambda r_1(\cos^2(\mu_1\omega_1) - r_1\sin^2(\mu_1\omega_1)\cos^2(\mu_1\omega_1) \\
&\quad -\alpha_1 r_2\cos^2(\mu_1\omega_1)\sin^2(\mu_2\omega_2)), \\
\dot{r}_2 &= 2\lambda r_2(\cos^2(\mu_2\omega_2) - \alpha_2 r_1\sin^2(\mu_1\omega_1)\cos^2(\mu_2\omega_2) \\
&\quad -r_2\sin^2(\mu_2\omega_2)\cos^2(\mu_2\omega_2)),
\end{aligned}
\tag{3}
$$

which is of the form

$$
\begin{aligned}
\dot{\boldsymbol{\Omega}} &= \mathbf{d} + \lambda\boldsymbol{\Theta}(\boldsymbol{\Omega}, \mathbf{r}), \\
\dot{\mathbf{r}} &= \lambda\mathbf{R}(\boldsymbol{\Omega}, \mathbf{r}),
\end{aligned}
\tag{4}
$$

with $\boldsymbol{\Omega} = \begin{pmatrix} \omega_1 \\ \omega_2 \end{pmatrix}$, $\mathbf{r} = \begin{pmatrix} r_1 \\ r_2 \end{pmatrix}$, $\mathbf{d} = \begin{pmatrix} 1 \\ 1 \end{pmatrix}$,

$$
\boldsymbol{\Theta}(\boldsymbol{\Omega}, \mathbf{r}) = \begin{pmatrix} \Theta_1(\boldsymbol{\Omega}, \mathbf{r}) \\ \\ \Theta_2(\boldsymbol{\Omega}, \mathbf{r}) \end{pmatrix} = \begin{pmatrix} \left(-\frac{1}{\mu_1}\right)(\sin(\mu_1\omega_1)\cos(\mu_1\omega_1) \\ -r_1\sin^3(\mu_1\omega_1)\cos(\mu_1\omega_1) \\ -\alpha_1 r_2\sin(\mu_1\omega_1)\cos(\mu_1\omega_1)\sin^2(\mu_2\omega_2)) \\ \left(-\frac{1}{\mu_2}\right)(\sin(\mu_2\omega_2)\cos(\mu_2\omega_2) \\ -\alpha_2 r_1\sin^2(\mu_1\omega_1)\sin(\mu_2\omega_2)\cos(\mu_2\omega_2) \\ -r_2\sin^3(\mu_2\omega_2))\cos(\mu_2\omega_2) \end{pmatrix},
$$

$$
\mathbf{R}(\boldsymbol{\Omega}, \mathbf{r}) = \begin{pmatrix} R_1(\boldsymbol{\Omega}, \mathbf{r}) \\ \\ R_2(\boldsymbol{\Omega}, \mathbf{r}) \end{pmatrix} = \begin{pmatrix} 2r_1(\cos^2(\mu_1\omega_1) \\ -r_1\sin^2(\mu_1\omega_1)\cos^2(\mu_1\omega_1) \\ -\alpha_1 r_2\cos^2(\mu_1\omega_1)\sin^2(\mu_2\omega_2)) \\ 2r_2(\cos^2(\mu_2\omega_2) \\ -\alpha_2 r_1\sin^2(\mu_1\omega_1)\cos^2(\mu_2\omega_2) \\ -r_2\sin^2(\mu_2\omega_2)\cos^2(\mu_2\omega_2)) \end{pmatrix}.
$$

2

For the current study we will assume that an invariant torus exists for (3) in the form

$$
\begin{aligned}
S \;=\; & \{(\mu_1\omega_1, \mu_2\omega_2, r_1, r_2) : r_1 = f(\mu_1\omega_1, \mu_2\omega_2), r_2 = g(\mu_1\omega_1, \mu_2\omega_2), \\
& (\mu_1\omega_1, \mu_2\omega_2) \in T^2\}.
\end{aligned}
\tag{5}
$$

Using the invariance of the graphs of $f(\mu_1\omega_1, \mu_2\omega_2)$ and $g(\mu_1\omega_1, \mu_2\omega_2)$ under the dynamics generated by (3) we have

$$
\begin{aligned}
\dot{\mathbf{r}} \;=\; & D_{\omega_1}\mathbf{F}(\mu_1\omega_1, \mu_2\omega_2)\dot{\omega}_1 + D_{\omega_2}\mathbf{F}(\mu_1\omega_1, \mu_2\omega_2)\dot{\omega}_2 \\
\;=\; & \lambda\mathbf{R}(\mathbf{\Omega}, \mathbf{F}(\mu_1\omega_1, \mu_2\omega_2)),
\end{aligned}
\tag{6}
$$

where $\mathbf{F} = \begin{pmatrix} f \\ g \end{pmatrix}$. Now, from (4),

$$
\begin{aligned}
\dot{\omega}_1 \;=\; & 1 + \lambda\Theta_1(\mathbf{\Omega}, \mathbf{F}(\mu_1\omega_1, \mu_2\omega_2)), \\
\dot{\omega}_2 \;=\; & 1 + \lambda\Theta_2(\mathbf{\Omega}, \mathbf{F}(\mu_1\omega_1, \mu_2\omega_2)).
\end{aligned}
\tag{7}
$$

We therefore substitute (7) into (6) to get the following quasilinear partial differential equation that $\mathbf{F}(\mu_1\omega_1, \mu_2\omega_2)$ must satisfy in order for its graph to be an invariant torus (See [8], [13]).

$$
\begin{aligned}
N(\mathbf{F}(\mu_1\omega_1, \mu_2\omega_2)) \;=\; & D_{\omega_1}\mathbf{F}(\mu_1\omega_1, \mu_2\omega_2)(1 + \lambda\Theta_1(\mathbf{\Omega}, \mathbf{F}(\mu_1\omega_1, \mu_2\omega_2))) \\
+ \; & D_{\omega_2}\mathbf{F}(\mu_1\omega_1, \mu_2\omega_2)(1 + \lambda\Theta_2(\mathbf{\Omega}, \mathbf{F}(\mu_1\omega_1, \mu_2\omega_2))) \\
- \; & \lambda\mathbf{R}(\mathbf{\Omega}, \mathbf{F}(\mu_1\omega_1, \mu_2\omega_2)) \;=\; 0.
\end{aligned}
\tag{8}
$$

For the remainder of the discussion, we make the following substitutions in order to simplify the notation in the equations.

$$
\begin{aligned}
\theta \;=\; & \mu_1\omega_1, \\
\phi \;=\; & \mu_2\omega_2.
\end{aligned}
$$

2 Bicubic Spline Collocation Method

We now use the method of collocation with B-splines to approximate the functions $r_1 = f(\theta, \phi)$ and $r_2 = g(\theta, \phi)$. We let

$$
\begin{aligned}
0 \;=\; & \theta_0 < \theta_1 < \ldots < \theta_n = 2\pi, \\
0 \;=\; & \phi_0 < \phi_1 < \ldots < \phi_m = 2\pi,
\end{aligned}
$$

be a uniform partition of the rectangle ranging over $[0, 2\pi]$ in the θ direction and $[0, 2\pi]$ in the ϕ direction where n and m are the number of knots in the θ and ϕ directions, respectively and $\Delta h = \theta_{i+1} - \theta_i = 2\pi/n$, $i = 0, \ldots, n-1$ and $\Delta k = \phi_{j+1} - \phi_j = 2\pi/m$, $j = 0, \ldots, m-1$. We seek bicubic spline surfaces of the form

$$
\begin{aligned}
r_{1,nm}(\theta, \phi) \;=\; & \sum_{i=-1}^{n+1} \sum_{j=-1}^{m+1} c_{ij} B_i(\theta) B_j(\phi), \\
r_{2,nm}(\theta, \phi) \;=\; & \sum_{i=-1}^{n+1} \sum_{j=-1}^{m+1} d_{ij} B_i(\theta) B_j(\phi),
\end{aligned}
\tag{9}
$$

3

where $\{B_{-1}(\theta), B_0(\theta), \ldots, B_{n+1}(\theta)\}$ are the B spline basis functions in the θ direction with knots θ_h, $h = 0, \ldots, n$ and $\{B_{-1}(\phi), B_0(\phi), \ldots, B_{m+1}(\phi)\}$ are the B spline basis functions in the ϕ direction with knots ϕ_k, $k = 0, \ldots, m$. The functions $B_i(\theta)$ are defined in Prenter[12] as follows by introducing four additional knots in each direction satisfying

$$
\begin{aligned}
\theta_{-2} < \theta_{-1} < \theta_0 = 0 \quad &\text{and} \quad \theta_{n+2} > \theta_{n+1} > \theta_n = 2\pi, \\
\phi_{-2} < \phi_{-1} < \phi_0 = 0 \quad &\text{and} \quad \phi_{n+2} > \phi_{n+1} > \phi_n = 2\pi,
\end{aligned}
\tag{10}
$$

$$
B_i(\theta) = \frac{1}{h^3}
\begin{cases}
(\theta - \theta_{i-2})^3 & \text{if } \theta \in [\theta_{i-2}, \theta_{i-1}] \\
h^3 + 3h^2(\theta - \theta_{i-1}) + 3h(\theta - \theta_{i-1})^2 - 3(\theta - \theta_{i-1})^3, \\
& \text{if } \theta \in [\theta_{i-1}, \theta_i] \\
h^3 + 3h^2(\theta_{i+1} - \theta) + 3h(\theta_{i+1} - \theta)^2 - 3(\theta_{i+1} - \theta)^3, \\
& \text{if } \theta \in [\theta_i, \theta_{i+1}] \\
0 & \text{otherwise.}
\end{cases}
\tag{11}
$$

The function $B_j(\phi)$ is defined similarly. These functions are twice continuously differentiable on the real line. We can therefore define $B_i'(\theta)$ and $B_i''(\theta)$ using the equations for $B_i(\theta)$. To compute the approximations $r_{1,nm}$ and $r_{2,nm}$ in (9) at the knots, we note that by substituting the knots θ_h and ϕ_k into the definitions of B, B', B'',

$$
B_i(\theta_h)B_j(\phi_k) =
\begin{cases}
16 & \text{if } h = i, k = j, \\
4 & \text{if } h = i-1, k = j \quad \text{or} \quad h = i, k = j-1 \\
& \text{or} \quad h = i, k = j+1 \quad \text{or} \quad h = i+1, k = j, \\
1 & \text{if } h = i-1, k = j-1 \\
& \text{or} \quad h = i-1, k = j+1 \\
& \text{or} \quad h = i+1, k = j-1 \\
& \text{or} \quad h = i+1, k = j+1,
\end{cases}
\tag{12}
$$

and $B_i(\theta_h)B_j(\phi_k) \equiv 0$ for $h \geq i+2, k \geq j+2$ and $h \leq i-2, k \leq j-2$.

The partial derivatives of the interpolants $r_{1,nm}(\theta, \phi)$, $r_{2,nm}(\theta, \phi)$ at the knots can be easily found using the first derivatives and the products $B_i'(\theta_h)B_j(\phi_k)$ and $B_i(\theta_h)B_j'(\phi_k)$ of the spline functions in the tables below.

4

	$(\theta_{i-1}, \phi_{j-1})$	(θ_{i-1}, ϕ_j)	$(\theta_{i-1}, \phi_{j+1})$
$B_i'(\theta)B_j(\phi)$	$\frac{3}{\Delta h}$	$\frac{12}{\Delta h}$	$\frac{3}{\Delta h}$
$B_i(\theta)B_j'(\phi)$	$\frac{3}{\Delta k}$	0	$-\frac{3}{\Delta k}$

	(θ_i, ϕ_{j-1})	(θ_i, ϕ_j)	(θ_i, ϕ_{j+1})
$B_i'(\theta)B_j(\phi)$	0	0	0
$B_i(\theta)B_j'(\phi)$	$\frac{12}{\Delta k}$	0	$-\frac{12}{\Delta k}$

	$(\theta_{i+1}, \phi_{j-1})$	(θ_{i+1}, ϕ_j)	$(\theta_{i+1}, \phi_{j+1})$
$B_i'(\theta)B_j(\phi)$	$-\frac{3}{\Delta h}$	$-\frac{12}{\Delta h}$	$-\frac{3}{\Delta h}$
$B_i(\theta)B_j'(\phi)$	$\frac{3}{\Delta k}$	0	$-\frac{3}{\Delta k}$

Table 1: Partial derivatives of the interpolants $r_{1,nm}(\theta,\phi), r_{2,nm}(\theta,\phi)$ at knots

Using the above information, the values of the approximations $r_{1,nm}$ and $r_{2,nm}$ at the knots can be expressed in terms of the parameters c_{ij} and d_{ij} as

$$
\begin{aligned}
r_{1,nm}(\theta_h, \phi_k) &= 16c_{h,k} + 4(c_{h-1,k} + c_{h,k-1} + c_{h,k+1} + c_{h+1,k}) \\
&\quad + c_{h-1,k-1} + c_{h-1,k+1} + c_{h+1,k-1} + c_{h+1,k+1}, \\
r_{2,nm}(\theta_h, \phi_k) &= 16d_{h,k} + 4(d_{h-1,k} + d_{h,k-1} + d_{h,k+1} + d_{h+1,k}) \\
&\quad + d_{h-1,k-1} + d_{h-1,k+1} + d_{h+1,k-1} + d_{h+1,k+1}.
\end{aligned}
\tag{13}
$$

A similar computation shows that the derivatives $\frac{\partial r_{1,nm}}{\partial \theta}(\theta_h, \phi_k)$, $\frac{\partial r_{1,nm}}{\partial \phi}(\theta_h, \phi_k)$, $\frac{\partial r_{2,nm}}{\partial \theta}(\theta_h, \phi_k)$ and $\frac{\partial r_{2,nm}}{\partial \phi}(\theta_h, \phi_k)$ at the knots have the following representation in terms of the parameters.

$$
\begin{aligned}
\frac{\partial r_{1,nm}}{\partial \theta}(\theta_h, \phi_k) &= \frac{3}{\Delta h}(c_{h+1,k+1} + 4c_{h+1,k} + c_{h+1,k-1} \\
&\quad - c_{h-1,k+1} - 4c_{h-1,k} - c_{h-1,k-1}), \\
\frac{\partial r_{1,nm}}{\partial \phi}(\theta_h, \phi_k) &= \frac{3}{\Delta k}(c_{h+1,k+1} - c_{h+1,k-1} + 4c_{h,k+1} \\
&\quad - 4c_{h,k-1} + c_{h-1,k+1} - c_{h-1,k-1}),
\end{aligned}
$$

$$\frac{\partial r_{2,nm}}{\partial \theta}(\theta_h, \phi_k) = \frac{3}{\Delta h}(d_{h+1,k+1} + 4d_{h+1,k} + d_{h+1,k-1}$$
$$-d_{h-1,k+1} - 4d_{h-1,k} - d_{h-1,k-1}),$$

$$\frac{\partial r_{2,nm}}{\partial \phi}(\theta_h, \phi_k) = \frac{3}{\Delta k}(d_{h+1,k+1} - d_{h+1,k-1} + 4d_{h,k+1}$$
$$-4d_{h,k-1} + d_{h-1,k+1} - d_{h-1,k-1}). \quad (14)$$

To apply the collocation method, we choose the collocation points to coincide with the knots and then substitute the nodal values $r_{1,nm}(\theta_h, \phi_k), r_{2,nm}(\theta_h, \phi_k)$ and their derivatives obtained in equations (13) and (14) into the partial differential equation (8). This results in the following system of $(n+1) \times (m+1)$ coupled nonlinear equations in $(n+3) \times (m+3)$ parameters c_{ij} and d_{ij}:

$$\left[\frac{3}{\Delta h}(c_{h+1,k+1} + 4c_{h+1,k} + c_{h+1,k-1} - c_{h-1,k+1}\right.$$
$$\left. -4c_{h-1,k} - c_{h-1,k-1}\right]((1 + \lambda\Theta_1(\mathbf{\Omega}, r_{1,nm}(\theta_h, \phi_k))))$$
$$+\left[\frac{3}{\Delta k}(c_{h+1,k+1} - c_{h+1,k-1} + 4c_{h,k+1} - 4c_{h,k-1}\right.$$
$$\left. +c_{h-1,k+1} - c_{h-1,k-1}\right](1 + \lambda\Theta_2(\mathbf{\Omega}, r_{1,nm}(\theta_h, \phi_k)))$$
$$-\lambda\mathbf{R}(\mathbf{\Omega}, r_{1,nm}(\theta_h, \phi_k)) = 0,$$
$$(15)$$

for $h = 0, \ldots, n$ and $k = 0, \ldots, m$.

3   Periodicity Conditions

The surface we are approximating is a closed one generated by two periodic closed curves. The spline model is therefore chosen so that it is closed in both the θ and ϕ directions. This is accomplished by repeating both the knots and the control vertices as follows.

$$(\theta_n, \phi_k) = (\theta_0, \phi_k), \quad 0 \le k \le m, \qquad (\theta_h, \phi_m) = (\theta_h, \phi_0), \quad 0 \le h \le n$$

$$c_{-1,j} = c_{n-1,j}$$
$$c_{n+1,j} = c_{1,j}, \qquad -1 \le j \le m+1$$

$$c_{i,-1} = c_{i,m-1}$$
$$c_{i,m+1} = c_{i,1}, \qquad -1 \le i \le n+1$$

$$c_{n,k} = c_{0,k}, \qquad 0 \le k \le m$$
$$c_{h,m} = c_{h,0}. \qquad 0 \le h \le n$$

Application of the above periodic boundary conditions reduces equation (13) to a nm $\times$ nm block-pentadiagonal matrix equation of the form

$$
\begin{bmatrix}
r_{1,nm}(0,0) \\
r_{1,nm}(0,1) \\
r_{1,nm}(0,2) \\
\vdots \\
r_{1,nm}((n-1),(m-2)) \\
r_{1,nm}((n-1),(m-1))
\end{bmatrix}
=
\begin{bmatrix}
D & B & 0 & \ldots & 0 & B \\
B & D & B & 0 & \ldots & 0 \\
0 & B & D & B & \ldots & 0 \\
\vdots & \vdots & \vdots & \vdots & \vdots & \vdots \\
0 & \ldots & 0 & B & D & B \\
B & 0 & \ldots & 0 & B & D
\end{bmatrix}
\begin{bmatrix}
c_{0,0} \\
c_{0,1} \\
c_{0,2} \\
\vdots \\
c_{(n-1),(m-2)} \\
c_{(n-1),(m-1)}
\end{bmatrix},
$$

(16)

where D and B are $m \times m$ pentadiagonal matrices with entries

$$
D =
\begin{bmatrix}
16 & 4 & 0 & \ldots & 0 & 4 \\
4 & 16 & 4 & 0 & \ldots & 0 \\
0 & 4 & 16 & 4 & \ldots & 0 \\
\vdots & \vdots & \vdots & \vdots & \vdots & \vdots \\
0 & \ldots & 0 & 4 & 16 & 4 \\
4 & 0 & \ldots & 0 & 4 & 16
\end{bmatrix},
$$

and

$$
B =
\begin{bmatrix}
4 & 1 & 0 & \ldots & 0 & 1 \\
1 & 4 & 1 & 0 & \ldots & 0 \\
0 & 1 & 4 & 1 & \ldots & 0 \\
\vdots & \vdots & \vdots & \vdots & \vdots & \vdots \\
0 & \ldots & 0 & 1 & 4 & 1 \\
1 & 0 & \ldots & 0 & 1 & 4
\end{bmatrix},
$$

with a similar matrix equation obtained for the approximation $r_{2,nm}$ by replacing the control points $c_{i,j}$ with $d_{i,j}$.

Similarly the system of partial derivatives of $r_{1,nm}$ in (14) reduce, after applying the periodic boundary conditions, to a block diagonal form

$$
\begin{bmatrix}
\frac{\partial r_{1,nm}}{\partial \theta}(0,0) \\
\frac{\partial r_{1,nm}}{\partial \theta}(0,1) \\
\frac{\partial r_{1,nm}}{\partial \theta}(0,2) \\
\vdots \\
\frac{\partial r_{1,nm}}{\partial \theta}((n-1),(m-2)) \\
\frac{\partial r_{1,nm}}{\partial \theta}((n-1),(m-1))
\end{bmatrix}
=
\begin{bmatrix}
0 & B & 0 & \ldots & 0 & -B \\
-B & 0 & B & 0 & \ldots & 0 \\
0 & -B & 0 & B & \ldots & 0 \\
\vdots & \vdots & \vdots & \vdots & \vdots & \vdots \\
0 & \ldots & 0 & -B & 0 & B \\
B & 0 & \ldots & 0 & -B & 0
\end{bmatrix}
\begin{bmatrix}
c_{0,0} \\
c_{0,1} \\
c_{0,2} \\
\vdots \\
c_{(n-1),(m-2)} \\
c_{(n-1),(m-1)}
\end{bmatrix},
$$

(17)

where B is a $m \times m$ diagonal matrix with entries

$$
B = \frac{3}{\Delta h}
\begin{bmatrix}
4 & 1 & 0 & \ldots & 0 & 1 \\
1 & 4 & 1 & 0 & \ldots & 0 \\
0 & 1 & 4 & 1 & \ldots & 0 \\
\vdots & \vdots & \vdots & \vdots & \vdots & \vdots \\
0 & \ldots & 0 & 1 & 4 & 1 \\
1 & 0 & \ldots & 0 & 1 & 4
\end{bmatrix},
$$

and

$$
\begin{bmatrix}
\frac{\partial r_{1,nm}}{\partial \phi}(0,0) \\
\frac{\partial r_{1,nm}}{\partial \phi}(0,1) \\
\frac{\partial r_{1,nm}}{\partial \phi}(0,2) \\
\vdots \\
\frac{\partial r_{1,nm}}{\partial \phi}((n-1),(m-2)) \\
\frac{\partial r_{1,nm}}{\partial \phi}((n-1),(m-1))
\end{bmatrix}
=
\begin{bmatrix}
D & B & 0 & \dots & 0 & B \\
B & D & B & 0 & \dots & 0 \\
0 & B & D & B & \dots & 0 \\
\vdots & \vdots & \vdots & \vdots & \vdots & \vdots \\
0 & \dots & 0 & B & D & B \\
B & 0 & \dots & 0 & B & D
\end{bmatrix}
\begin{bmatrix}
c_{0,0} \\
c_{0,1} \\
c_{0,2} \\
\vdots \\
c_{(n-1),(m-2)} \\
c_{(n-1),(m-1)}
\end{bmatrix},
$$

$$(18)$$

where D and B are $m \times m$ diagonal matrices with entries

$$
D = \frac{12}{\Delta k}
\begin{bmatrix}
0 & 1 & 0 & \dots & 0 & -1 \\
-1 & 0 & 1 & 0 & \dots & 0 \\
0 & -1 & 0 & 1 & \dots & 0 \\
\vdots & \vdots & \vdots & \vdots & \vdots & \vdots \\
0 & \dots & 0 & -1 & 0 & 1 \\
1 & 0 & \dots & 0 & -1 & 0
\end{bmatrix},
$$

and

$$
B = \frac{3}{\Delta k}
\begin{bmatrix}
0 & 1 & 0 & \dots & 0 & -1 \\
-1 & 0 & 1 & 0 & \dots & 0 \\
0 & -1 & 0 & 1 & \dots & 0 \\
\vdots & \vdots & \vdots & \vdots & \vdots & \vdots \\
0 & \dots & 0 & -1 & 0 & 1 \\
1 & 0 & \dots & 0 & -1 & 0
\end{bmatrix},
$$

with similar expressions obtained for the partial derivative approximations $\frac{\partial r_{2,nm}}{\partial \theta}$, $\frac{\partial r_{2,nm}}{\partial \phi}$ by replacing the control points $c_{i,j}$ with $d_{i,j}$.

4 MATLAB solution

We now describe the algorithmic details involved in computing the bicubic B-spline coefficients c_{ij} and d_{ij} by setting up an appropriate objective function to be mimimized using MATLAB's nonlinear minimization subroutine. Our objective function simply computes the "residual error": the difference between the derivative of the approximations $r_{1,nm}$, $r_{2,nm}$ and the derivatives $\dot{r}_1$, $\dot{r}_2$ respectively as given by the system (3) which is equivalent to the partial differential equation given by (8). Substituting equations (16),(17), and (18) into the partial differential equation system (15), we reduce it to a 2nm system of coupled nonlinear equations in 2nm parameters c_{ij} and d_{ij}. The determining equations can now be written as

$$
R_{1,hk}(A) = \frac{\partial r_{1,nm}}{\partial \theta}(h,k)((1 + \lambda \Theta_1(\boldsymbol{\Omega}, \mathbf{r}(h,k)))) + \frac{\partial r_{1,nm}}{\partial \phi}(h,k)(1 + \lambda \Theta_2(\boldsymbol{\Omega}, \mathbf{r}(h,k)))
$$

$$
- \lambda \mathbf{R_1}(\boldsymbol{\Omega}, \mathbf{r}(h,k)) = 0,
$$

$$
R_{2,hk}(A) = \frac{\partial r_{2,nm}}{\partial \theta}(h,k)((1 + \lambda \Theta_1(\boldsymbol{\Omega}, \mathbf{r}(h,k)))) + \frac{\partial r_{2,nm}}{\partial \phi}(h,k)(1 + \lambda \Theta_2(\boldsymbol{\Omega}, \mathbf{r}(h,k)))
$$

$$-\lambda \mathbf{R_2}(\mathbf{\Omega}, \mathbf{r}(h, k)) = 0,$$

(19)

for $h = 0, 1, \ldots, n$, $k = 0, 1, \ldots, m$, where $\mathbf{A} = [\mathbf{c}; \mathbf{d}]$ with $\mathbf{c} = (c_{-1,-1}, c_{-1,0}, \ldots, c_{n+1,m+1})^T$ and $\mathbf{d} = (d_{-1,-1}, d_{-1,0}, \ldots, d_{n+1,m+1})^T$. Equation (19) can then be used to find an approximation for the vector $\mathbf{A}$ by a minimization process, such as

$$\min_{c,d} \sum_{k=1}^{2nm} |R_k(A)|^2.$$

(20)

We use MATLAB's `fsolve` command to solve the system of nonlinear equations for the parameters. For an initial guess, we fix the following parameters for this case study:

$$\alpha_1 = 0.2, \ \alpha_2 = 0.4, \ \mu_1 = 1, \ \mu_2 = 1.414,$$

(21)

and take the first approximation to the radii as

$$r_{1,nm} = 3.53, \ r_{2,nm} = 1.18.$$

(22)

We note that the matrix form of equation (16) is

$$Ac = r,$$

(23)

with the matrix A being nonsingular. That is, system (16) has a unique solution and consequently, the collocation approximate (9)satisfying the periodic boundary conditions is uniquely defined. We can therefore solve (23) by substituting the initial guess for $r_{1,nm}$ and $r_{2,nm}$ as 3.53 and 1.18 respectively into the right hand side of (23)to obtain the vector c of the unknown parameters c_{ij} as

$$c = A^{-1}r.$$

(24)

A similar calculation yields the initial vector d of the unknown parameters d_{ij}.

5   Optimization Issues

For the first few runs, we coded the objective function and called up the `fsolve` optimization routine without supplying the sparsity pattern of the Jacobian. This worked well for small values of λ but as the strength of coupling increased, we had to increase the size of the knot domain for getting a good approximation as well as for the optimization to terminate successfully. Increasing the size of the knot domain for bigger values of λ slowed down the optimization considerably. Computationally, the model proved expensive even for $\lambda = 0.5$, which appeared to require a 40 by 40 knot domain for a reasonably good approximation.

The residual error for any point in the knot domain depends only on the nine surrounding parameters and therefore has very few non-zero partial derivatives. The Jacobian is sparse with well-structured blocks of non-zero elements. The computational cost of finite differencing, which MATLAB uses to approximate the Jacobian, can therefore be reduced significantly, if we can supply

9

the structure of the Jacobian to MATLAB. This is done by setting `JacobPattern` to 'on' in `options`. This was our first improvement to the code. With this enhancement the results were encouraging for λ between 0.1 and 1.0: The number of function evaluations per iteration dropped significantly (for example, for $\lambda = 0.5$ with a 40 by 40 knot domain, the number of evaluations dropped from 3202 to just 32 per iteration!),and the time required for the optimization to successfully terminate reduced considerably. The following table summarizes these results. Unfortunately, supplying the

$\lambda = 0.5,$ knots=40		
Implementation	Normalized Residual Error	Time for Optimization
Jacobian Structure Unspecified	2.26395e-007	4.0188e+003 secs
Jacobian Structure Specified	2.33638e-007	41.3750 secs

Jacobian Sparsity Pattern appears to be insufficient for λ bigger than or equal to 1.0, which require bigger knot domains for achieving the required accuracy. For these coupling strengths, running the code generates an 'Out of Memory' output in MATLAB. The figures below for $\lambda = 1.0$ & 2.0 were generated with a 50 by 50 knot domain and the optimization was incomplete. Although unoptimized, the bicubic spline surface appears to capture the surface generated by numerical integration of the full system as shown in figures (3) and (4)below.

6 Results

We present here the results of running our code for four different values of the coupling parameter. In each case, the error trends were computed between the numerically integrated angle-radial equations, equation (4)using the MATLAB ode45 solver, and the approximate system of phase equations on the torus, given by

$$\dot{\Omega} = \mathbf{d} + \lambda \Theta(\Omega, \mathbf{r_{nm}}(\theta, \phi)),$$
$$\mathbf{r} = \mathbf{r_{nm}}(\theta, \phi). \tag{25}$$

We set the error tolerance in these computations to 10^{-8} and tabulated the results. First, we consider the case $\lambda = 0.1$. We ran the code for three different sizes of the knot domain starting with 20 knots in each of the θ and ϕ directions. Figure (1)shows the full and approximate system integration for the case $\lambda = 0.1$.

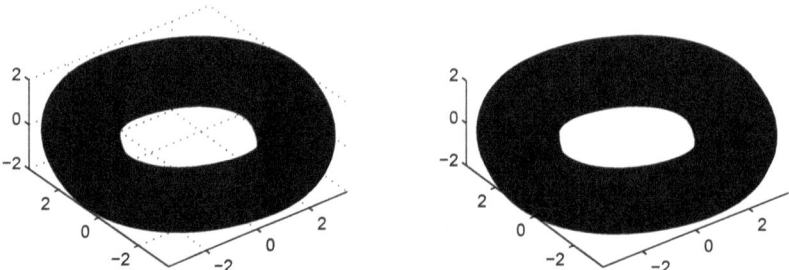

Figure 1: Bicubic approximation (left)and numerically integrated Van der Pol (right) for $\lambda = 0.1$ with a 30 by 30 knot domain

Table (3) shows the results of changing the number of knots keeping $\lambda = 0.1$ fixed. The third row shows the time T1 which represents the sum of the seconds it takes to create the necessary matrices in the main program plus the time it takes to evaluate once the function called by the optimization subroutine. T2 in seconds is the sum of T1 and the time it takes to run the optimization subroutine `fsolve` in MATLAB. The last row gives the normed residual error in each case.

Table 2: Summary table for $\lambda = 0.1$ showing timings and residual error.

$\lambda = 0.1$			
Knots	20	30	40
T1(seconds)	0	0.0160	0.0630
T2(seconds)	7.0620	13.3290	38.8750
Normed Residual Error	1.92718e-010	9.35666e-010	6.38028e-009

Figure (2) represents the $\lambda = 0.6$ case. We observe some deforming of the torus but the bicubic surface appears to be similar to that generated by the MATLAB's ode45 solver.

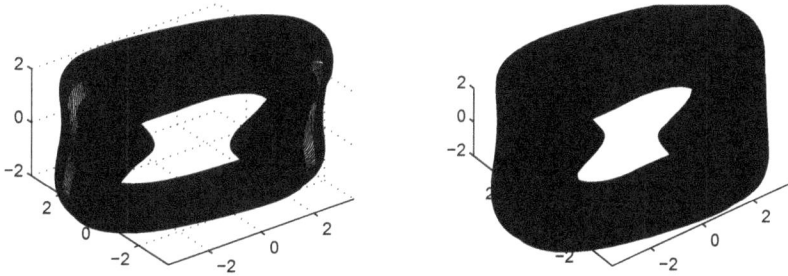

Figure 2: Bicubic approximation (left)and numerically integrated Van der Pol (right) for $\lambda = 0.6$ with a 45 by 45 knot domain

Table 3: Summary table for $\lambda = 0.6$ showing timings and residual error.

$\lambda = 0.6$			
Knots	40	45	50
T1(seconds)	0.0620	0.0780	0.1410
T2(seconds)	68.1250	80.7190	265.6710
Normed Residual Error	8.00207e-011	9.18135e-010	7.72686e-008

As mentioned in the previous section, for values of $\lambda \geq 1.0$ the optimization did not terminate successfully due to insufficient number of knots. Figures (3) and (4) depict two such cases. We note that as the strength of coupling increase, the inner sides of the invariant torus get closer and eventually connect with each other. Again, the results appear to be consistent.

7   Conclusions

This case study presents an alternate approach to approximating the invariant torus of the coupled Van der Pol oscillator. The bicubic B-spline collocation method in conjunction with the vectorization capabilities offered by the MATLAB processing system provides us with the tools for developing a significant time saving optimization algorithm for efficiently computing the approximate periodic

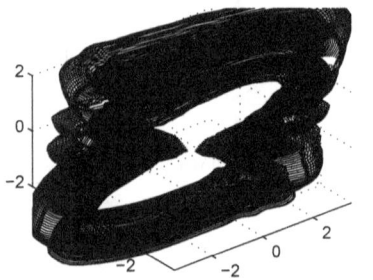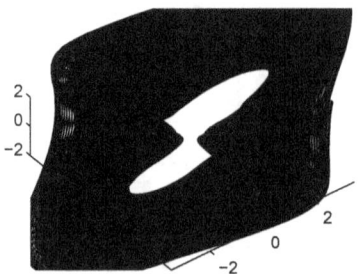

Figure 3: Bicubic approximation (left)and numerically integrated Van der Pol (right) for $\lambda = 1.0$ with a 50 by 50 knot domain

surface. Comparisons of the present approach with the MATLAB numerical integration of the full system of coupled oscillators indicate that the method demonstrated in this paper is promising. For strong nolinear coupling, computer memory appears to be the only limitation.

8   Disclaimer

Certain commercial software products are identified in this paper in order to adequately specify the computational procedures. Such identification does not imply recommendation or endorsement by the National Institute of Standards and Technology nor does it imply that the software products identified are necessarily the best available for the purpose.

References

[1] Bogoliubov, N. N., Mitropolsky, Y. A., *Asymptotic Methods in the Theory of Non-Linear Oscillations*, Gordon and Breach, New York, 1961.

[2] Dag, I., Irk, D.,and Sahin, A., 'B-spline Collocation Methods for Numerical Solutions of the Burger's Equation',*Mathematical Problems in Engineering* **5**, 2005, 521-538.

[3] Dyksen, W., Houstis, E., Lynch, R., and Rice, J.,'The performance of the collocation and Galerkin methods with Hermite bicubics',*SIAM Journal of Numerical Analysis* **21**, 1984, 695-715.

[4] Ge, T., and Leung, A. Y. T.,'Construction of Invariant Torus Using Toeplitz Jacobian Matrices/Fast Fourier Transform Approch',*Nonlinear Dynamics* **15**, 1998, 283-305.

[5] Gilsinn, D. E., 'Asymptotic Approximations of Integral Manifolds', *SIAM J. Appl. Math.*, **47**, 5, 1987, 929-940.

[6] Gilsinn,D.E., 'Constructing Invariant Tori for Two Weakly Coupled van der Pol Oscillators', *Nonlinear Dynamics* **4**, 1993, 289-308.

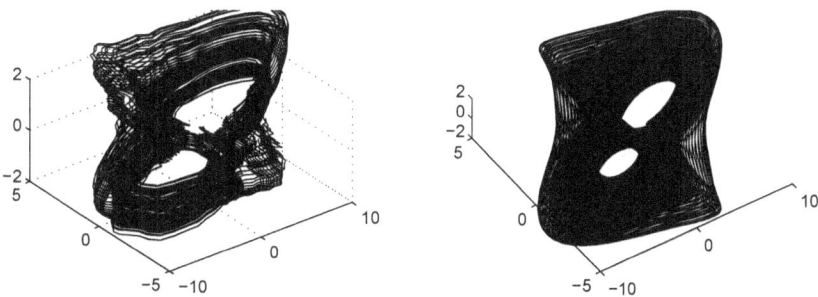

Figure 4: Bicubic approximation (left)and numerically integrated Van der Pol (right) for $\lambda = 2.0$ with a 50 by 50 knot domain

[7] Gilsinn,D.E., 'Constructing Galerkin's Approximations of Invariant Tori Using MACSYMA', *Nonlinear Dynamics* **8**, 1995, 269-305.

[8] Guckenheimer, J., and Holmes, P., *Nonlinear Oscillations, Dynamical Systems, and Bifurcations of Vector Fields*, Springer-Verlag, New York, 1983, 130 -138.

[9] Hale, J. K., 'Integral manifolds of perturbed differential equations', *Ann. of Math.*, **73**, 1961, 496-531.

[10] Hale, J. K., *Ordinary Differential Equations*, Wiley-Interscience, New York, 1969.

[11] Lu,F., and Milios, E. E., 'Optimal spline fitting to planar shape',*Signal Processing* **37**, 1994,129-140.

[12] Prenter,P.M., *Splines and Variational Methods*, John Wiley & Sons, 1975, 78 - 87.

[13] Wiggins,S., *Introduction to Applied Nonlinear Dynamical Systems and Chaos*, Springer-Verlag, New York, 1990, 193 - 204.

A   B-spline Code for Approximate Torus

```
function Main_VanderPol_Coupled
%MAIN_VANDERPOL_COUPLED - This primary function creates the diagonal matrices
%D and B for each of the matrix equations approximating the functions r_1 and r_2
%and their derivatives at the knots in both the theta and phi directions, calls the subfunctions
%for computing the optimized B-spline coefficients and plots the bicubic
%spline surfaces.
%
%AUTHOR:
%   Sita Ramamurti
%   Mathematics Program
%   Trinity Washington University
%   125 Michigan Avenue, N.E.
%   Washington, D.C. 20017-1094
%
%*****************************************************************
```

13

```
global lambda meu1 meu2 a alph
global m n h k delta1 delta2 nm np1 mp1 np1mp1 mp4 np3 np2 np4 mp3 mp2 np3mp3 np5mp5
global theta phi thetavector phivector
global r1_nm dr1dtheta_nm dr1dphi_nm
global r2_nm dr2dtheta_nm dr2dphi_nm
global thetadot phidot
global r1dot r2dot
global R1 R2
global B1red B2red B3red Jpat Jred
global c d
global tim2 tim3

%enter the following parameters
meu1=1.0;%input('enter the parameter meu1,meu1=');
meu2=1.414;%input('enter the parameter meu2,meu2=');
a=0.2;%input('enter the parameter a,a=');
alph=0.4;%input('enter the parameter alph,alph=');

%enter the following inputs
lambda=input('enter the parameter lamda,lambda=');
n=input('enter harmonics n, n=');
m=input('enter harmonics m, m=');

np1=n+1;mp1=m+1;np2=n+2;mp2=m+2;np3=n+3;mp3=m+3;
np1mp1=np1*mp1;np3mp3=np3*mp3;
nm=n*m;

tim=clock;

theta=zeros(np3,1);
phi=zeros(mp3,1);
B1red=zeros(nm,nm);
B2red=zeros(nm,nm);
B3red=zeros(nm,nm);
Jpat=zeros(2*nm,2*nm);

% mesh specified by {theta= meu1*omega1_i:i=1,2,...,n+5}& {phi=meu2*omega2_j:i=1,2,...,m+5}
delta1=2*pi/n;
delta2=2*pi/m;

h=2:np2;
theta(h)=(h-2)*delta1;

k=2:mp2;
phi(k)=(k-2)*delta2;

%creating the B1redmatrix
%create the matrix block B1
```

```
B1=zeros(m,m); JB1=zeros(m,m);
h=0;
%the first row of the block
B1(rindex(h,0),rindex(h,0))=16;
B1(rindex(h,0),rindex(h,1))=4;
B1(rindex(h,0),rindex(h,m-1))=4;

JB1(rindex(h,0),rindex(h,0))=1;
JB1(rindex(h,0),rindex(h,1))=1;
JB1(rindex(h,0),rindex(h,m-1))=1;
%the last row of the block
B1(rindex(h,m-1),rindex(h,0))=4;
B1(rindex(h,m-1),rindex(h,m-2))=4;
B1(rindex(h,m-1),rindex(h,m-1))=16;

JB1(rindex(h,m-1),rindex(h,0))=1;
JB1(rindex(h,m-1),rindex(h,m-2))=1;
JB1(rindex(h,m-1),rindex(h,m-1))=1;
%for the intermediate rows
for k=1:m-2;
B1(rindex(h,k),rindex(h,k))=16;
B1(rindex(h,k),rindex(h,k-1))=4;
B1(rindex(h,k),rindex(h,k+1))=4;

JB1(rindex(h,k),rindex(h,k))=1;
JB1(rindex(h,k),rindex(h,k-1))=1;
JB1(rindex(h,k),rindex(h,k+1))=1;
end

%create the matrix block B2
B2=zeros(m,m); JB2=zeros(m,m);
h=0;
%the first row of the block
B2(rindex(h,0),rindex(h,0))=4;
B2(rindex(h,0),rindex(h,1))=1;
B2(rindox(h,0),rindex(h,m-1))=1;

JB2(rindex(h,0),rindex(h,0))=1;
JB2(rindex(h,0),rindex(h,1))=1;
JB2(rindex(h,0),rindex(h,m-1))=1;
%the last row of the block
B2(rindex(h,m-1),rindex(h,0))=1;
B2(rindex(h,m-1),rindex(h,m-2))=1;
B2(rindex(h,m-1),rindex(h,m-1))=4;

JB2(rindex(h,m-1),rindex(h,0))=1;
JB2(rindex(h,m-1),rindex(h,m-2))=1;
JB2(rindex(h,m-1),rindex(h,m-1))=1;
```

```
for k=1:m-2;
B2(rindex(h,k),rindex(h,k))=4;
B2(rindex(h,k),rindex(h,k-1))=1;
B2(rindex(h,k),rindex(h,k+1))=1;

JB2(rindex(h,k),rindex(h,k))=1;
JB2(rindex(h,k),rindex(h,k-1))=1;
JB2(rindex(h,k),rindex(h,k+1))=1;
end

%now create the reduced matrix B1red using the above blocks
%for the first m rows
B1red(rindex(0,0:m-1),rindex(0,0):rindex(0,m-1))=B1;
B1red(rindex(0,0:m-1),rindex(1,0):rindex(1,m-1))=B2;
B1red(rindex(0,0:m-1),rindex(m-1,0):rindex(m-1,m-1))=B2;

Jred(rindex(0,0:m-1),rindex(0,0):rindex(0,m-1))=JB1;
Jred(rindex(0,0:m-1),rindex(1,0):rindex(1,m-1))=JB2;
Jred(rindex(0,0:m-1),rindex(m-1,0):rindex(m-1,m-1))=JB2;

%for the last m rows
B1red(rindex(m-1,0:m-1),rindex(0,0):rindex(0,m-1))=B2;
B1red(rindex(m-1,0:m-1),rindex(m-2,0):rindex(m-2,m-1))=B2;
B1red(rindex(m-1,0:m-1),rindex(m-1,0):rindex(m-1,m-1))=B1;

Jred(rindex(m-1,0:m-1),rindex(0,0):rindex(0,m-1))=JB2;
Jred(rindex(m-1,0:m-1),rindex(m-2,0):rindex(m-2,m-1))=JB2;
Jred(rindex(m-1,0:m-1),rindex(m-1,0):rindex(m-1,m-1))=JB1;

%for the middle rows
for h=1:m-2;
        B1red(rindex(h,0:m-1),rindex(h,0:m-1))=B1;
        B1red(rindex(h,0:m-1),rindex(h-1,0:m-1))=B2;
        B1red(rindex(h,0:m-1),rindex(h+1,0:m-1))=B2;

        Jred(rindex(h,0:m-1),rindex(h,0:m-1))=JB1;
        Jred(rindex(h,0:m-1),rindex(h-1,0:m-1))=JB2;
        Jred(rindex(h,0:m-1),rindex(h+1,0:m-1))=JB2;
end
clear B1 B2 JB1 JB2

%Jacpat
Jpat(2*nm,2*nm)=single(0);
Jpat(1:nm,1:nm)=Jred;
Jpat(1:nm,nm+1:2*nm)=Jred;
Jpat(nm+1:2*nm,1:nm)=Jred;
Jpat(nm+1:2*nm,nm+1:2*nm)=Jred;
```

```
clear Jred;

%creating the B2redmatrix
%create the matrix block B1
B1=zeros(m,m);
h=0;
%the first row of the block
B1(rindex(h,0),rindex(h,0))=12/delta1;
B1(rindex(h,0),rindex(h,1))=3/delta1;
B1(rindex(h,0),rindex(h,m-1))=3/delta1;

%the last row of the block
B1(rindex(h,m-1),rindex(h,0))=3/delta1;
B1(rindex(h,m-1),rindex(h,m-2))=3/delta1;
B1(rindex(h,m-1),rindex(h,m-1))=12/delta1;

%for the intermediate rows
for k=1:m-2;
B1(rindex(h,k),rindex(h,k))=12/delta1;
B1(rindex(h,k),rindex(h,k-1))=3/delta1;
B1(rindex(h,k),rindex(h,k+1))=3/delta1;

end

%create the matrix block B2
B2=zeros(m,m);
h=0;
%the first row of the block
B2(rindex(h,0),rindex(h,0))=-12/delta1;
B2(rindex(h,0),rindex(h,1))=-3/delta1;
B2(rindex(h,0),rindex(h,m-1))=-3/delta1;

%the last row of the block
B2(rindex(h,m-1),rindex(h,0))=-3/delta1;
B2(rindex(h,m-1),rindex(h,m-2))=-3/delta1;
B2(rindex(h,m-1),rindex(h,m 1))=-12/delta1;

%for the intermediate rows
for k=1:m-2;
B2(rindex(h,k),rindex(h,k))=-12/delta1;
B2(rindex(h,k),rindex(h,k-1))=-3/delta1;
B2(rindex(h,k),rindex(h,k+1))=-3/delta1;

end

%now create the reduced matrix Bred using the above blocks
%for the first m rows
B2red(rindex(0,0:m-1),rindex(1,0):rindex(1,m-1))=B1;
```

```
B2red(rindex(0,0:m-1),rindex(m-1,0):rindex(m-1,m-1))=B2;

%for the last m rows
B2red(rindex(m-1,0:m-1),rindex(0,0):rindex(0,m-1))=B1;
B2red(rindex(m-1,0:m-1),rindex(m-2,0):rindex(m-2,m-1))=B2;

%for the middle rows
for h=1:m-2;
        B2red(rindex(h,0:m-1),rindex(h-1,0:m-1))=B2;
        B2red(rindex(h,0:m-1),rindex(h+1,0:m-1))=B1;
end

clear B1 B2;

%creating the B3redmatrix
%create the matrix block B1
B1=zeros(m,m);
h=0;
%the first row of the block
B1(rindex(h,0),rindex(h,1))=12/delta2;
B1(rindex(h,0),rindex(h,m-1))=-12/delta2;

%the last row of the block
B1(rindex(h,m-1),rindex(h,0))=12/delta2;
B1(rindex(h,m-1),rindex(h,m-2))=-12/delta2;

%for the intermediate rows
for k=1:m-2;
    B1(rindex(h,k),rindex(h,k-1))=-12/delta2;
    B1(rindex(h,k),rindex(h,k+1))=12/delta2;
end

%create the matrix block B2
B2=zeros(m,m);
h=0;
%the first row of the block
B2(rindex(h,0),rindex(h,1))=3/delta2;
B2(rindex(h,0),rindex(h,m-1))=-3/delta2;

%the last row of the block
B2(rindex(h,m-1),rindex(h,0))=3/delta2;
B2(rindex(h,m-1),rindex(h,m-2))=-3/delta2;

%for the intermediate rows
for k=1:m-2;
    B2(rindex(h,k),rindex(h,k-1))=-3/delta2;
    B2(rindex(h,k),rindex(h,k+1))=3/delta2;
end
```

```
%now create the reduced matrix Bred using the above blocks
%for the first m rows
B3red(nm,nm)=single(0);
B3red(rindex(0,0:m-1),rindex(0,0):rindex(0,m-1))=B1;
B3red(rindex(0,0:m-1),rindex(1,0):rindex(1,m-1))=B2;
B3red(rindex(0,0:m-1),rindex(m-1,0):rindex(m-1,m-1))=B2;

%for the last m rows
B3red(rindex(m-1,0:m-1),rindex(0,0):rindex(0,m-1))=B2;
B3red(rindex(m-1,0:m-1),rindex(m-2,0):rindex(m-2,m-1))=B2;
B3red(rindex(m-1,0:m-1),rindex(m-1,0):rindex(m-1,m-1))=B1;

%for the middle rows
for h=1:m-2;
        B3red(rindex(h,0:m-1),rindex(h,0:m-1))=B1;
        B3red(rindex(h,0:m-1),rindex(h-1,0:m-1))=B2;
        B3red(rindex(h,0:m-1),rindex(h+1,0:m-1))=B2;
end

clear B1 B2;

%now for the optimization

%initialize the parameters c and d
c=zeros(np3mp3,1);
d=zeros(np3mp3,1);

%initialize the approximation vectors r1_nm & r2_nm
r1_nm=zeros(nm,1);
r2_nm=zeros(nm,1);
phivector=zeros(nm,1);
thetavector=zeros(nm,1);
thetadot=zeros(nm,1); phidot=zeros(nm,1);
r1dot=zeros(nm,1); r2dot=zeros(nm,1);

%initialize the residuals R1 and R2
R1=zeros(nm,1);
R2=zeros(nm,1);

%initialize the partial derivative vectors dr1dtheta dr1dphi dr2dtheta
%dr2dphi
dr1dtheta_nm=zeros(nm,1);
dr1dphi_nm=zeros(nm,1);
dr2dtheta_nm=zeros(nm,1);
dr2dphi_nm=zeros(nm,1);

%initialize the matrices A and b for getting the initial conditions
```

```
b1=zeros(nm,1);
b2=zeros(nm,1);
b=zeros(nm,2);

cred=zeros(nm,1);
dred=zeros(nm,1);
A=zeros(nm,2);
A_bar=zeros(nm,2);

%reshape the theta1 theta and phi vectors to make each of them a n*m vector
phivector=repmat(phi(2:mp1,1),n,1);%copies the whole vector n times
thetavector=kron(theta(2:np1,1),ones(m,1));%copies each element m times

b1(1:nm,1)=3.53;
b2(1:nm,1)=1.18;
cred=inv(B1red)*b1;
dred=inv(B1red)*b2;

A=[cred dred];

%load Jpat
%'JacobPattern',Jpat,

tim1=etime(clock,tim);
options=optimset('Display','iter','TolX',1e-8,'LargeScale','on','JacobPattern',Jpat,'MaxFunEvals',1C
[A_bar,obj_val]=fsolve(@myobjfun,A,options);

tim3=etime(clock,tim);
disp('Set up time for F')
tim2
disp('Total time including optimization')
tim3

% use periodicity to get the whole set of c and d
%put in the optimized c & d values into the cij,dij vectors

for k=0:n-1;
c(index(k,0:m-1))=A_bar(k*m+1:(k+1)*m,1);
d(index(k,0:m-1))=A_bar(k*m+1:(k+1)*m,2);
end

%put in the periodic values of the parameters c
%for i=0:m-1;
    c(index(n,0:m-1))= c(index(0,0:m-1));
    d(index(n,0:m-1))= d(index(0,0:m-1));
    %end
%for i=0:n-1;
    c(index(0:n-1,m))= c(index(0:n-1,0));
```

```
      d(index(0:n-1,m))= d(index(0:n-1,0));
      %end
c(index(-1,-1))= c(index(n-1,m-1));

c(index(-1,mp1))= c(index(n-1,1));
c(index(np1,-1))= c(index(1,m-1));

c(index(np1,mp1))= c(index(1,1));

d(index(-1,-1))= d(index(n-1,m-1));

d(index(-1,mp1))= d(index(n-1,1));
d(index(np1,-1))= d(index(1,m-1));

d(index(np1,mp1))= d(index(1,1));

c(index(n,m))= c(index(0,0));
c(index(0,m))= c(index(0,0));

d(index(n,m))= d(index(0,0));
d(index(0,m))= d(index(0,0));

c(index(n-1,m))= c(index(n-1,0));
c(index(n,m-1))= c(index(0,m-1));
c(index(n,mp1))= c(index(n,1));
c(index(np1,m))= c(index(1,m));

d(index(n-1,m))= d(index(n-1,0));
d(index(n,m-1))= d(index(0,m-1));
d(index(n,mp1))= d(index(n,1));
d(index(np1,m))= d(index(1,m));

%for i=0:m;
    c(index(-1,0:m))= c(index(n-1,0:m));
    c(index(np1,0:m))= c(index(1,0:m));

    d(index(-1,0:m))= d(index(n-1,0:m));
    d(index(np1,0:m))= d(index(1,0:m));
    %end

%for i=0:n;
    c(index(0:n,-1))= c(index(0:n,m-1));
    c(index(0:n,mp1))= c(index(0:n,1));

    d(index(0:n,-1))= d(index(0:n,m-1));
    d(index(0:n,mp1))= d(index(0:n,1));
    %end
```

```
%plot_surface

%substitute rapprox into thetadot and integrate to get thetcap(t)
tspan=0:pi/100:2*pi;
thet0=[0 0]';
[t,thetcap]=ode45(@thetaODEdotBspline_coup,tspan,thet0);
thet1cap=thetcap(:,1);
thet2cap=thetcap(:,2);

%subsitute thetcap vector to get the corresponding rcap vector
s=length(thet1cap);
r1cap=zeros(s,1);
for i=1:s;
      r1cap(i)=r1approxfun_Bspline(thet1cap(i),thet2cap(i));
end

w=length(thet2cap);
r2cap=zeros(w,1);
for i=1:w;
     r2cap(i)=r2approxfun_Bspline(thet1cap(i),thet2cap(i));
end

tspan=0:pi/100:4*pi;
z0=[3.53 0 1.18 0]';
[t,z1]=ode45(@vdpolODEsystemeq_coup,tspan,z0);
r1ML=z1(:,1);
theta1ML=z1(:,2);
r2ML=z1(:,3);
theta2ML=z1(:,4);

%plot the full system integration and the phase equation integration
numb=input('enter figure # numb, numb=');
figure(numb);
title({'lambda=',lambda,'harmonics=',n});
p=length(thet1cap);
q=length(thet2cap);
x=zeros(p,q);y=zeros(p,q);z=zeros(p,q);
for i =1:p
for j=1:q
x(i,j)=r1cap(i)*cos(thet1cap(i))+r2cap(j)*cos(thet2cap(j))*cos(thet1cap(i));
y(i,j)=r1cap(i)*sin(thet1cap(i))+r2cap(j)*cos(thet2cap(j))*sin(thet1cap(i));
z(i,j)=r2cap(j)*sin(thet2cap(j));
end
end

subplot(2,2,1);
plot3(x,y,z);
grid on;
```

22

```
axis([-3.5 3.5 -3.5 3.5 -2 2]);
p=length(theta1ML);
q=length(theta2ML);
x=zeros(p,q);y=zeros(p,q);z=zeros(p,q);
for i =1:p
for j=1:q
x(i,j)=r1ML(i)*cos(theta1ML(i))+r2ML(j)*cos(theta2ML(j))*cos(theta1ML(i));
y(i,j)=r1ML(i)*sin(theta1ML(i))+r2ML(j)*cos(theta2ML(j))*sin(theta1ML(i));
z(i,j)=r2ML(j)*sin(theta2ML(j));
end
end

subplot(2,2,2);
plot3(x,y,z);
axis([-3.5 3.5 -3.5 3.5 -2 2]);

%************************************************************************
function loc=rindex(i,j)
%RINDEX - This function converts an array matrix to a single column of values.
%
%Input:
%    i - matrix row
%    j - matrix column
%
%Output:
%   loc - column vector of values
%
%AUTHOR:
%   Sita Ramamurti
%   Mathematics Program
%   Trinity Washington University
%   125 Michigan Avenue, N.E.
%   Washington, D.C. 20017-1094
%
%************************************************************************
global m
loc=i*m+j+1;


%************************************************************************
% The Objective Function
function y=myobjfun(A)
%MYOBJFUN - This function sets up the appropriate objective function to be
%minimized using MATLAB's nonlinear minimization subroutine.
%
%Input:
%    A - this is the vector [c; d]of the B-spline coefficients
%
%Output:
```

```
%    y - this is the vector of "residual errors"
%
%AUTHOR:
%    Sita Ramamurti
%    Mathematics Program
%    Trinity Washington University
%    125 Michigan Avenue, N.E.
%    Washington, D.C. 20017-1094
%
%**************************************************************************
global lambda meu1 meu2 a alph
global m n nm np1 mp1 np1mp1 np3mp3 np5mp5
global theta phi thetavector phivector
global N M Np Mp Npp Mpp
global r1_nm dr1dtheta_nm dr1dphi_nm
global r2_nm dr2dtheta_nm dr2dphi_nm
global r1_lowb r1_upb r1_leftb r1_rightb
global r2_lowb r2_upb r2_leftb r2_rightb
global r1dot_nm r2dot_nm
global thetadot phidot
global r1dot r2dot
global R1 R2
global B1red B2red B3red
global tim2

tim=clock;

% use the above B matrices to define the approximations r1_nm and r2_nm
% at the knots theta(3) to theta(n+3) and
% at phi(3) to phi(m+3)
r1_nm=B1red*A(:,1);
r2_nm=B1red*A(:,2);

%compute the approximations dr1dtheta_nm & dr2dtheta_nm
dr1dtheta_nm=B2red*(meu1*A(:,1));
dr2dtheta_nm=B2red*(meu1*A(:,2));
%compute the approximations dr1dphi_nm & dr2dphi_nm
dr1dphi_nm=B3red*(meu2*A(:,1));
dr2dphi_nm=B3red*(meu2*A(:,2));
%compute the residuals
thetadot=1+lambda.*(-(1/meu1).*(sin(thetavector).*cos(thetavector)-...
                      r1_nm.*sin(thetavector).^3.*cos(thetavector)-...
                      a.*r2_nm.*sin(thetavector).*cos(thetavector).*sin(phivector).^2));
phidot=1+lambda.*(-(1/meu2).*(sin(phivector).*cos(phivector)-...
                      alph.*r1_nm.*sin(thetavector).^2.*sin(phivector).*...
                      cos(phivector)-r2_nm.*sin(phivector).^3.*cos(phivector)));

r1dot=lambda.*2.*r1_nm.*(cos(thetavector).^2-r1_nm.*sin(thetavector).^2.*cos(thetavector).^2-...
```

```matlab
                a.*r2_nm.*cos(thetavector).^2.*sin(phivector).^2);
r2dot=lambda.*2.*r2_nm.*(cos(phivector).^2-alph.*r1_nm.*sin(thetavector).^2.*cos(phivector).^2-...
                r2_nm.*cos(phivector).^2.*sin(phivector).^2);

%compute the r1&r2dot matrices and the residuals
r1dot_nm=dr1dtheta_nm.*thetadot+dr1dphi_nm.*phidot;
r2dot_nm=dr2dtheta_nm.*thetadot+dr2dphi_nm.*phidot;
R1=r1dot_nm-r1dot;
R2=r2dot_nm-r2dot;

y=[R1;R2];

tim2=etime(clock,tim);
%**********************************************************************
function loc=index(i,j)
%INDEX - This function converts an array matrix to a single column of values.
%
%Input:
%   i - matrix row
%   j - matrix column
%
%Output:
%   loc - column vector of values
%
%AUTHOR:
%   Sita Ramamurti
%   Mathematics Program
%   Trinity Washington University
%   125 Michigan Avenue, N.E.
%   Washington, D.C. 20017-1094
%
%**********************************************************************
global mp3
loc=(i+1)*mp3+2+j;


%**********************************************************************
%integration of the phase equation to get thetacap
function thetaprime=thetaODEdotBspline_coup(t,thet)
%THETAODEDOTBSPLINE - This function substitutes the bicubic spline
%approximations for r_1 and r_2 into the Van der Pol system equations for the derivatives
%of omega_1 and omega_2.
%Input:
%   t - a vector specifying the interval of integration
%   thet - a vector specifying the knot location in the theta and phi
%   directions
%
%Output:
%   thetaprime - vector of derivatives of omega_1 and omega_2
```

```
%
%AUTHOR:
%    Sita Ramamurti
%    Mathematics Program
%    Trinity Washington University
%    125 Michigan Avenue, N.E.
%    Washington, D.C. 20017-1094
%
%************************************************************************
global lambda meu1 meu2 a alph

if thet(1)<0;
        thet(1)=-thet(1);
    end

if thet(2)<0;
        thet(2)=-thet(2);
    end

r1=r1approxfun_Bspline(thet(1),thet(2));
r2=r2approxfun_Bspline(thet(1),thet(2));
thetaprime=[1+lambda*(-(1/meu1)*(sin(meu1*thet(1))*cos(meu1*thet(1))-r1*sin(meu1*thet(1))^3*...
            cos(meu1*thet(1))-...
            a*r2*sin(meu1*thet(1))*cos(meu1*thet(1))*sin(meu2*thet(2))^2));

            1+lambda*(-(1/meu1)*(sin(meu2*thet(2))*cos(meu2*thet(2))-alph*r1*sin(meu1*thet(1))^2*...
            sin(meu2*thet(2))*...
            cos(meu2*thet(2))-r2*sin(meu2*thet(2))^3*cos(meu2*thet(2))))];


%van der pol oscillator in polar coordinates
%************************************************************************
function RThetaprime=vdpolODEsystemeq_coup(t,z1);
%VDPOLODESYSTEMEQ_COUP - This function sets up the system of coupled Van
%der Pol oscillators in polar form.
%
%Input:
%    t - a vector specifying the interval of integration
%    z1 - a vector of initial conditions
%
%Output:
%    RTthetaprime - a column vector of equations corresponding to the system
%
%AUTHOR:
%    Sita Ramamurti
%    Mathematics Program
%    Trinity Washington University
%    125 Michigan Avenue, N.E.
```

26

```
%   Washington, D.C. 20017-1094
%
%************************************************************************
global lambda meu1 meu2 a alph

RThetaprime=...
[lambda*2*z1(1)*(cos(meu1*z1(2))^2-z1(1)*sin(meu1*z1(2))^2*cos(meu1*z1(2))^2-...
                a*z1(3)*cos(meu1*z1(2))^2*sin(meu2*z1(4))^2);
1+lambda*(-(1/meu1))*(sin(meu1*z1(2))*cos(meu1*z1(2))-z1(1)*sin(meu1*z1(2))^3*cos(meu1*z1(2))-...
          a*z1(3)*sin(meu1*z1(2))*cos(meu1*z1(2))*sin(meu2*z1(4))^2);
lambda*2*z1(3)*(cos(meu2*z1(4))^2-alph*z1(1)*sin(meu1*z1(2))^2*cos(meu2*z1(4))^2-...
                z1(3)*cos(meu2*z1(4))^2*sin(meu2*z1(4))^2);
1+lambda*(-(1/meu2))*(sin(meu2*z1(4))*cos(meu2*z1(4))-alph*z1(1)*sin(meu1*z1(2))^2*sin(meu2*z1(4))*.
        cos(meu2*z1(4))-z1(3)*sin(meu2*z1(4))^3*cos(meu2*z1(4)))];


%************************************************************************
function r1hat=r1approxfun_Bspline(t,s)
%R1APPROXFUN_BSPLINE - This function constructs the bicubic spline
%surface r_1 using the optimized spline coefficients.
%
%Input:
%   t - location of the knot in the theta direction
%   s - location of the knot in the phi direction
%
%Output:
%   r1hat - function value of r_1 at the (t,s) knot
%
%AUTHOR:
%   Sita Ramamurti
%   Mathematics Program
%   Trinity Washington University
%   125 Michigan Avenue, N.E.
%   Washington, D.C. 20017-1094
%
%************************************************************************
global n delta1 m delta2 np3mp3 np4 mp3 mp4 np3
global theta phi
global c

%initialize the spline matrix B
Bi=zeros(np3,1);
Bj=zeros(mp3,1);

%find out in which interval 't' falls
klo=2; khi=n+2;
while (khi-klo)>1;
    k=fix((khi+klo)/2);
    if theta(k)>t;
```

```
        khi=k;
    else
        klo=k;
    end
end

%compute the B spline at 't'
j=klo;
h=delta1;

Bi(j-1)=(1/h^3)*(theta(j+1)-t)^3;
Bi(j)  =(1/h^3)*(h^3+3*h^2*(theta(j+1)-t)+3*h*(theta(j+1)-t)^2-3*(theta(j+1)-t)^3);
Bi(j+1)=(1/h^3)*(h^3+3*h^2*(t-theta(j))+3*h*(t-theta(j))^2-3*(t-theta(j))^3);
Bi(j+2)=(1/h^3)*(t-theta(j))^3;

%find out in which interval 's' falls
klo=2; khi=m+2;
while (khi-klo)>1;
    k=fix((khi+klo)/2);
    if phi(k)>s;
        khi=k;
    else
        klo=k;
    end
end

%compute the B spline at 's'
v=klo;
h=delta2;

Bj(v-1)=(1/h^3)*(phi(v+1)-s)^3;
Bj(v)  =(1/h^3)*(h^3+3*h^2*(phi(v+1)-s)+3*h*(phi(v+1)-s)^2-3*(phi(v+1)-s)^3);
Bj(v+1)=(1/h^3)*(h^3+3*h^2*(s-phi(v))+3*h*(s-phi(v))^2-3*(s-phi(v))^3);
Bj(v+2)=(1/h^3)*(s-phi(v))^3;

Bivector=zeros(np3mp3,1);
Bjvector=zeros(np3mp3,1);

Bivector=kron(Bi(1:np3,1),ones(mp3,1));
Bjvector=repmat(Bj(1:mp3,1),np3,1);
r1hat=c'*(Bivector.*Bjvector);

%*************************************************************************
function r2hat=r2approxfun_Bspline(t,s)
%R2APPROXFUN_BSPLINE - This function constructs the bicubic spline
%surface r_2 using the optimized spline coefficients.
%
%Input:
```

```
%   t - location of the knot in the theta direction
%   s - location of the knot in the phi direction
%
%Output:
%   r2hat - function value of r_2 at the (t,s) knot
%
%AUTHOR:
%   Sita Ramamurti
%   Mathematics Program
%   Trinity Washington University
%   125 Michigan Avenue, N.E.
%   Washington, D.C. 20017-1094
%
%****************************************************************************
global n delta1 m delta2 np3mp3 np4 mp3 mp4 np3
global theta phi
global d

%initialize the spline matrix B
Bi=zeros(np3,1);
Bj=zeros(mp3,1);

%find out in which interval 't' falls
klo=2; khi=n+2;
while (khi-klo)>1;
    k=fix((khi+klo)/2);
    if theta(k)>t;
        khi=k;
    else
        klo=k;
    end
end

%compute the B spline at 't'
j=klo;
h=delta1;

Bi(j-1)=(1/h^3)*(theta(j+1)-t)^3;
Bi(j)  =(1/h^3)*(h^3+3*h^2*(theta(j+1)-t)+3*h*(theta(j+1)-t)^2-3*(theta(j+1)-t)^3);
Bi(j+1)=(1/h^3)*(h^3+3*h^2*(t-theta(j))+3*h*(t-theta(j))^2-3*(t-theta(j))^3);
Bi(j+2)=(1/h^3)*(t-theta(j))^3;

%find out in which interval 's' falls
klo=2; khi=m+2;
while (khi-klo)>1;
    k=fix((khi+klo)/2);
    if phi(k)>s;
        khi=k;
```

```
        else
            klo=k;
        end
end

%compute the B spline at 's'
v=klo;
h=delta2;

Bj(v-1)=(1/h^3)*(phi(v+1)-s)^3;
Bj(v)  =(1/h^3)*(h^3+3*h^2*(phi(v+1)-s)+3*h*(phi(v+1)-s)^2-3*(phi(v+1)-s)^3);
Bj(v+1)=(1/h^3)*(h^3+3*h^2*(s-phi(v))+3*h*(s-phi(v))^2-3*(s-phi(v))^3);
Bj(v+2)=(1/h^3)*(s-phi(v))^3;

Bivector=zeros(np3mp3,1);
Bjvector=zeros(np3mp3,1);

Bivector=kron(Bi(1:np3,1),ones(mp3,1));
Bjvector=repmat(Bj(1:mp3,1),np3,1);
r2hat=d'*(Bivector.*Bjvector);
```